Mark My Words

Poems
by
Tonn Pastore

Words Floating on the Trout River appeared in Florida Speaks, 2014.

Edited by Lynn Skapyak Harlin
Cover Art and Design by Oscar Senn

Published by Hidden Owl, LLC,
Hiddenowl.com

ISBN 978-0-9962371-2-3

Printed in the United States

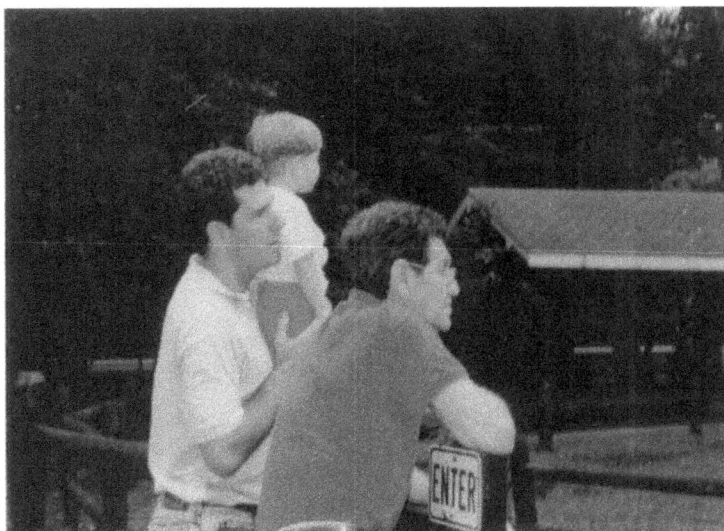

For my son Mark

My words won't change circumstances

    Change any minds

Won't make time go any faster

    Just know I will never leave you behind.

Contents

I Will Have My Day

All the things that could have been
if I had been ready when
time to take a chance came then,
I'd be different today.

All the things that would have been
all those things that will be when
all you people listen then,
I will have my way.

Everything will fall in place
there will be a change of pace
problems then will be erased,
I will have my day.

Mirrors in Limbo

Eyes wide but focused low
won't look around to see.
Aware scared spared so far
hammer will come down.

Each man a mirror.
Reflections everywhere.
Does he see himself
in each of these men?

The echoes of his wounds
bounce off these walls.
Muted cries of victims
are slowly absorbed.

Redundant reelection
different day same day
same frame of reference.
Ground hog day from Hell.

Within walls hope falls.
Inside the heart starts
to draw new lines to build
more walls to hold in hope.

Hope escapes like the smoke
from a smuggled cigarette
odor remains evidence gone.
Fire up another, every day.

Another book read, if only
done during school, if, if, if.
Upper lip stiff as a window sill.
Windows found only in eyes.

Respite visits, phone calls out.
Pencil sketches the world seen.
Two dimensional, too shallow
to deepen any feelings.

Feelings. Walled in, caged
rage, malaise, brazen hatred
worst of the world worn down
drowning all except love.

Doesn't Get Any Better

Driving down Third Street
eight pm eating Taco Bell
with my nine-year old.
Thirty-five mph
five windows open
seventy-five degrees
a Florida night
three blocks from the ocean.
It doesn't get any better
than this for me.

Driving down same road
alone eating less greasy
food missing my boy
missing my heart.
It's away.
He's away.
I'm away
way, way down
the road.

Clear Brown Eyes

Gotta run, gotta race,
     gotta make a better pace.
Gotta get there can't be late,
     can't leave him standing by the gate.

He wants to see his Daddy there
     no excuses, doesn't care.
Business phone calls, traffic snares,
     can't be late, I wouldn't dare.

"Why is ice so cold?" he asks.
     This is one of several tasks
he wants me to explain to him, why
     it is cats don't swim.

What is Mad Cow disease?
     What is it makes the breeze?
Does ten yards make for a first down?
     When will I be back in town?

He looks at me and wants to know,
     why it is I have to go?
He wants me there all year long
     wants me to correct when he's wrong.

His eyes are brown, but they're so clear
     mine I try to hide the fear
I won't be there when it counts
     the miles a distance I can't surmount.

So, love will carry through the air,
     on a fiber optic pair
of cables that will go two ways,
     'till I return next Saturday.

5

Limbo Lingering Along

It has all been disrupted.
The American dream of
being educated, starting a career,
falling in love, getting married
having a baby, raising the baby
a child, the teenager, young adult
being educated starting a...
All stopped.

No grandpa to be for me
no ballgame with a boy
no chance to send the seed
into the future.
Maybe for the best?
Maybe being a 22nd century
American won't be so great?

I can learn to accept it.
Time allows for that.
Instead of getting easier
seems worse, harder
seems abnormal a new normal
can't slip into my psyche securely.
Denial prevails until it doesn't.

The five stages thing may work
for death, but what about this?
This is limbo lingering along.
He's a 'bird without a song.'
My boy is The Birdman.
He sang when he shouldn't.
He sings because he has to.

Fracking

Isn't pressurized water
or chemicals that release
the feelings
a tap that pokes pain
captured collected capped
gas caustic, eyes burn
tap water ignites
little earthquakes
acid reflux of the earth
hydraulic heartburn.
Fear flies
love lost.

My Heart Is Broken

My heart is broken.
I carry it around in pieces in a bag.
It's a non-recyclable one from Publix.
My wife would not approve of the plastic.

Pieces rattle around inside it.
I fear they will slip out, fall to the ground
as I carry them around place to place.
So, sometimes I leave them home
or in the trunk of my car.

"I'm fine." I say. I'm not fine.
My heart is broken.
Love comes in fragments now.
Emotions are scattered in shards.
Feelings now burst
like a can of soda dropped
on a garage floor. A mess.

My heart is broken.
Like a watch that can't keep time
it stays quiet, no tick, no tock
helpful twice a day but not much
more than jewelry adorning a wrist.
I appear okay but if anyone looks
they see it is a broken watch.

Schpilkes

Nerves.
I am a bundle of them.
In a day when energy
is in demand
I hold enough in my hand
for an entire land.

Depressants that could
fell a horse of course
do little else to me, then to
increase the release
which gives me no peace
is the cause for
more than one deceased.

I realize very little
but the barrier is brittle.
Surrounds the shell
appears to be well.
Inside of me is the plea
to be free of the care
to beware of another's stare.

My stomach makes a noise
something is poised
to rear its ugly head
with something I dread.
This simple chore
never bothered me before.

It's something else
inside myself.
It's not a pain within my brain
which makes the body strain
toward something ignited
it makes me excited.

Words Floating on the Trout River

At the top of the Dames Point
first look is to the left
up the Trout River.
City pokes into the horizon
like a monopoly board piece,
future cruise ship terminal
a denuded smear below.

The look is to see if the shanty boat
can be spotted at it's dock.
Never can but do it every time.
Each time feel
excitement, anticipation,
rejection, acceptance,
give, take, ebb, flow.

The St. Johns lets the tide go
back upstream for miles.
Classroom with a tin top
floats atop this water,
forum of feedback faster than the river
a story ending becomes closer
often with a fiery sunset
always with a smoky cloud of love.

Bridges find the shanty boat
so can a cruise up the Pablo.
Across the "Ditch"
too slow though,
always rushing, just in time
to bring the work, the words,
present tense, point of view,
first person or third
there to hear how others
float their special words
on the shanty boat on the river.

The Alchemist

Burning
Like a cigarette in an ash tray
Lynn burns bobbing her head
with the rhythm of a new story.

Burning
Hotter like a drag on cigarette
smoke is sucked inward until
third draft of same chapter has not
been changed. Exhale exclaims emotions
in a thin grey cloud of instruction.

Burning
Flame that lights Lynn's life
must be ready. Match must
reach the end of her fuel
fire feelings she will reveal.

Burning
Inside is a tiny cauldron.
Love unleashed when
corrections are made
sentences restructured
characters completed
stories shown not told.

Burning
Her hair burns white hot
atop head full of knowledge.
It's been sucking in thick
exhaling thin vapor cloud.
An alchemist creates change
cloud to concrete to love.

Mosey

I mosey, meander
amble on through
I'm never in a hurry
so why the hell are you?

I walk a little slowly
don't care when I arrive
neighborhood wandering
helps me feel more alive.

Don't care what is behind me
do look to the sides
enjoying all the scenery
blue up in the skies.

Brick road that is golden
pavers underfoot
road rise up to meet me
help the foot I put.

I poke, I mope
don't have to hurry up to cope
leave a little early
habit learned when I smoked dope.

Like a dog out on his walk
check the bushes through
analyze what's on the wind
sniff a butt or two.

Mosey meander
amble on through
never in a hurry
why the hell are you?

The Old Church

The wooden church pews
are worn with the stories
in the hands of the many
who've steadied themselves
filing in filing out.

The pads on the kneelers
squish from the weight
of the pain pressed down
during prayers thrown up
to the man on the cross.

Mother Mary extends
her arms to love the children.
The ladies with the veils of
lace atop their heads shuffle
quietly to their familiar
place beneath her gaze.

The morning sun pulls
through the stained glass
magnifies the simply drawn
saints. Bartholomew,
Thomas, Phillip and James.

The mass early morning
minus the music moves
along at a pace. Readings
are concise, consecration
the focus. Communion carries
everyone forward through the day.

The Owl and the Salesman

The telephone screams
like a teething baby.
Our study of the wind,
interrupted.
We listen to the trees
hope to hear the owl.
The phone salesman says
he will sell us insurance
from the storm
which is sure to come
blow our house down.
We told him we couldn't
talk right now
an owl was preparing
to tell us about the breeze.

A Bad Day at Bikram Yoga?

I lost my cross today.
Icon on a golden chain
surrounded me for forty years
it's gone.
My fear is also missing
an open feeling now rings my neck.

Symbol of identification
a statement, says I believe in the man
who was nailed to the wood.
My cross was nailed to me long ago.
In New Jersey, it's just jewelry.
A family gift thrown over our heads
like a Hawaiian lei.
Does the symbol feel as light as flowers
or as heavy as wood dragged up the hill?

Cross at my feet, I stood on one leg
bowing my back, balancing,
stretching, reaching for more.
Homage, union, counting my heartbeats,
feeling the drumbeat rhythm of my soul.

Forgot left it behind, came back it was gone.
Missing, vanished into thin air.
Someone else picked it up
their cross to bear now.
Will it be as heavy as a tree
or as light as a lei?
Measured in more than carats
I am lighter today.

The Box Fan

Whistling in its own wind
box fan pushes us along.
A breeze seems gentle and fine
slips over our shoulders.
Our sails raise.
We propel into each other
now by the added wind speed
the jib is out.
Her barometric pressure dropping.
This gale, this storm whirls
us around and around the room
through the window.
We knock down trees
crush the cars
destroy the trailer park.
Lying back,
we survey the damage
wait for the TV crews to come
conduct the interview.

Presbyopia

An emergency
brought us together
to touch, to smell.
Smells trigger memories
poignant, pained.
Nose does a better job
than anything else.
These smells are aromas
memories that
erase the bad ones.

Last time we were this close
I saw you crystal clear
counted each of your eyelashes.
Today someone smudged
Vaseline over my lens.
You are soft focus, an old
Hollywood movie.
I reached for my new glasses
atop my head to
see you more clearly.
Instead I decided to let
my nose see you
all by itself.

My Attraction Is Distracted

My attraction is distracted by the memory of your kiss
altering my schedule just might make me miss
chance to get another, another liquid dish,
I want to taste your lips again today.

My attraction is distracted by the voice I get to hear
low and lovely sound that lingers in my ears
voice that brings the words I don't hear in my career
I want to hear them said to me today.

My attraction is distracted by the beating of my heart
its racing like I'm running but it's long before the start.
I'm breathing kind of heavy like a watcher in the dark
I want to hear your voice again today.

My attraction is distracted by the memory of your face.
An image in my mind won't find any to replace
beauty of your gaze is like a gift of special grace
I want to see your eyes again today.

My attraction is distracted by the memory of your scent.
A slight intoxication from the time that we spent
sitting close together the time just came and went.
I want to smell your neck again today.

Julia's Sonnet

To lay on a beach made empty by rain
others chased away by the dimming gloom.
How can I make all this happen again
like privacy of being in one's own room?
Two with the sand and the sea and the air
sounds of their laughter all their own.
Two with their hands and their hearts to share
talking together about all they have known.
To lay on a couch hear words by the Bard
tasting raspberry sherbet on each other's lips.
It was the letting go that turned out to be hard
feelings fall forward in romantic courtships.
To court her today to dream of her tomorrow
no one less than Shakespeare today I will borrow.

Cellophane Blinders

The sound explodes from the kitchen
like a wood chipper eating a tree.
She smiles and says, "Sorry."
Green smoothies she calls them.
Green, like the mat at a driving range.

A prepared pile of pills await each day.
Smoothies, supplements surge in her system,
twenty-first century communion of hosts.
No tan (a taboo), tight, toned, turns men's
heads like a twist top on a bottle of beer.

She always looked straight ahead
wore designer blinders to avoid the eyes.
Boys have been looking since junior high,
women wait until she passes
then their heads do the sign of the cross.

Blonde mane still long not shorn into
an appropriate bob. A bit of botox,
bottle of Clairol, rumba and spinning
because she is no longer mistaken
for her daughter's sister.

She wonders now. *Are they still looking?*
Today her blinders are made of cellophane.
She peeks over her shoulder,
hips wiggle more, jeans worn tight over legs
as long as an Obama speech.

Smiles at what she sees in her man's eyes.
"Want me to make you a smoothie?" she asks.
"Sure," he says watching her bend over
to reach the blender, "Sure."

Mosquito Bites

I wish I were a mosquito
    lighting atop her thigh.
I would take a bite of her
    then away I'd fly.

Then she'd want to touch the spot
    I had just been biting.
Now I'm nibbling on her ear
    it just looked so inviting.

As she would begin to spin
    I'd float without a care
then I'd park and leave my mark
    on her beautiful derriere.

Although she might just think of me
    as nothing but a pest
I leave behind a feeling that
    really is the best.

The feeling that I'm describing
    really can't be matched
It's the wonderful sensation
    when the itch is scratched.

Cuban Emerald

I sip from you
hummingbird who
drinks from flowers
my lips are wings
vibrate, taste, take
treat myself to you
get the energy
sip you like
a hummingbird
who drinks from flowers
over and over again.

Bickering

What is it about the bickering that bothers you, baby?
    She bubbled to me on the phone.
Does dickering the details of Yes, No, Maybe
    make you want to hang up and be alone?

Can quibbling cause chaos in couples these days
    can it create the start of a rift?
Does debate do us in diabolical ways?
    Do we adjust or die adrift?

Who else will ask the hard questions of you
    if it isn't the love of your life?
Who else will care if the answers are true
    between those known as man and wife.

So what if you land on a point of great friction
    sound squeaks like nails on a board
beware only if it becomes an addiction
    the anger becomes its own reward.

Getting used to feeling as bad as we do
    is a dangerous road to go down
becomes so easy to deny what is true
    might as well just get out of town.

Are there things one can say can't be taken back?
    Are there lines can't be crossed
are there feelings just should stay inside of us
    or escape, have everything lost?

Kiss Kiss

Kiss kiss, nibble nibble
      chew chew, mmm.
Tickle tickle, scratch scratch
      Rub rub, Vrroooom.

Off we go once again
      travel to the stars
flying at the speed of WOW
      zooming right by Mars.

First, I think I'll touch you here
      then I'll touch you there.
What happens to this button when
      I give it special care?

Roll over for me now my dear
      your head over the side
put the pillow under here
      spread your wings out wide.

Around the bed we go tonight
      twelve hours on the clock
three o'clock is going well
      but six o'clock'll rock.

We sink into the mattress down
      fall in the clouds below
swirl with the wind under our feet
      fly around real slow.

Hover like a hummingbird
      beat my wings real fast
longer that we stay aloft
      lingering will last.

This will last a long, long time
      chewing and the kissing.
you're the one now in my life
      always has been missing.

And Now the Weather (a Cinquain)

Break out
those old Nehru
jackets and the love beads
it's going to be *in the sixties*
today

Dog Haiku

As you go through life
remember to stop and pee
on all the flowers

The Cat's Meow

The cat meowed smiled
it looked like it ate a bird
up burped a lizard

Attila the Hun

Attila's a Hun, when he's all done
     he's got what he came to get.
He's pillaged and plundered your feelings
     asunder, all you get is regret.

I guess it was fun with Attila the Hun
     it's not everyday that you meet,
the leader of a Chinese Mongol horde,
     that you just can't beat.

When you've been done by Attila the Hun
     your body is no longer your own.
Your ego's deflated, your body is sated,
     you're best to be left alone.

Attila's a honey when you give him money,
     he'll perform for you pay-per-view.
Give him a reward, he'll show you his sword,
     he'll do it right on cue.

Once it's begun, Attila's the one to finish
     what he's gotten started.
No army can stop his invasion of you,
     he'll leave you broken hearted.

A Day at the Mall

Wait, wait for it.
Inhale now.
Take in the wake
      a comet tail
           a vapor trail
                 a wedding train.
To sup on the stardust
which follows her is to
visit a heavenly place
I inhale for an instant take her in me
know her for a moment
see her past, her present, her future.

Want to turn and share
what I know
what will happen for her
but the flash doesn't last
I turn she disappears
into the crowd.

I forget her future
her perfume
sweet aroma of the soap
she uses everyday
stardust is gone
wait, wait for it.

Nuclear Waste Disposal

She sprinkled
plutonium
on the photograph
hoped to destroy
the memory
of the man
she can't
remember
to forget.
She doesn't know
which one
has a longer
half-life.

Black Cocktail Dresses

Misfitted jeans and a cool leather jacket
her laugh lit me up like a smoke on the stairs.
"Let me show you a picture.
I'm in love with the photographer
come look at the coolest thing here.
I know you from somewhere
are you from the Oldest City?
Al Letson's my hero.
I've got a motorcycle, it's not pretty."

She wasn't kidding, duct taped seat
all I wanted to do was ride on the back
reverse a role in a fantasy for fun.
She writes, laughs, takes me for a ride,
then drops me at a curb
leaves in a wake of exhaust.

Then I talked to every black
cocktail dress in the room.
Six and one half black cocktail dresses
not one lit me up
not one made me laugh
not one owned a bike
not one knew what Oscar Wilde
meant when he said,
"All bad poetry comes from true feelings."

Gnats

In the south,
they're called
"No See-Ums"
New Jersey, Gnats.
When I opened
the car door
this morning
one was pulled in.
It buzzed around
helpless
needing to connect
with the warmth
of my face.

I felt like a gnat
sucked into a world
where I don't want to be.
Enclosed in a cabin
sweeping me away
without any control
over my destination.

Subjected to a swat
still fail to stay away
from the face of
the one who can
slap my psyche
squish my soul?

Spun inside a capsule
weightless as astronauts
on the space station
spin in orbit
circle the sights,
suspended in cabin
until it comes
to the stop light.
Propelled into windshield
splattered
wonder why
I didn't see it coming.

Mons Venus

She works the other nine to five shift
just another working girl on casual Friday.
The secretary pool in here is more of a puddle.
Hard working, she'll give you the shirt
off her back for three minutes, hand it to you
as her jeans fall to the floor. Bored, she bends
over my knee. "No, Brandy is not my real name.
Her? Oh, she's all upset because the guy
was squeezing her girlfriend's tits.
Me? I like guys, most of the time."

"They all hate men," says a guy with a gut and
a gator on his hat. The far wall is moving
it's a ceiling to floor mirror in front of a couch.
Six naked girls writhe atop six fully clothed guys.
Six carefully cut coifs, more grooming below
than above, a pubic poodle parlor.

Two metal bars horizontally pierce her clitoris.
They invite some doll sized trapeze artist
to swing on them from front to back.
"They hurt when I had 'em put in, now they feel great.

"This tattoo is for my daughter. She's two.
Her name is Brianne. I guess there are about
fifty girls here tonight, it is Friday. Yah, this place
is different, it's as famous as any in Tampa.
Go on touch me, its okay, touch me right there."
"Is this your last live nerve?" I ask.
"No, I just have an itch."

Butt Beach

There's a certain beauty
      about even the most popular
      beach when nobody is on it.

The only tracks are those of birds,
      the sun shines off the water
      not the faces of Coppertoned tourists.

Some people might say it looks
      like an ash tray
      in a living room after a party

If I weren't in such a good mood
      I might think
      they were right.

Chemtrails

Like white paint
bleeding into blue poster board
chemtrails expand across the sky.
Color sifts, drifts, dissipates drops.
Look skyward and wonder
some ask why we don't look under
blanket of deception that is so clear
yet completely covers the truth.

Each day of the week criss-crossing
planes crop dust our astrosphere
covering us with a pollen of lies.
Lies that hide lies, lies that surprise
lies we don't want to know.

All politics are local.
Banks are our friends.
Our food is safe.
Presidents are qualified.
The soft downy wool is being
pulled over our eyes.

But it is soft, light as air
it seems only fair to accept
what they tell us.
Why would they lie?
The future for us
is as high as that sky.

Lies cover Ferguson
Fallujah and Philadelphia.
Dust deadens our resolve
removes our revolution.
Disbelief bleeds into the landscape.

Not the Greatest Thing to Hit Kansas

Like James Dickey's stewardess
I was sucked out the window
the airplane of my life.
Every dream dropped down
like a Terry Gilliam cartoon.

I dived into the shallowness
the two dimensional world.
Zappa's slime pool portal
everywhere else
anywhere that isn't here.

Time stopped being linear
the fall from cloud to earth came
so hard. I bounced, floated, fell again.
Landed face first, flat.

Earth insisted on unconditional love.
My surrender incomplete
all distractions welcomed
ADOL, attention deficit, "Oh look."

The weight sometimes
lifted by helium tethers
but the gas escaped
fear was a heavy weight.

During this fall
more than clothes peeled away
empathy, care, enthusiasm
touch, love fled, too.

Unlike Dickey's stewardess
on this fall I was not
the greatest thing
to ever hit Kansas.

While Watching an Old Movie

I watch the handle pull.
Box of Marlboro drops.
Thirty-two years gone
gut response the same.
Back at a cigarette machine
a club in nineteen eighty-four.
Cellophane shiny, smooth
Can feel it now
smell the tobacco
from the discarded wrap
when the box is open.
Heart beat a bit faster
inhaled reflexively
nothing to smell
nothing to touch.
Memory drifts away
like deep exhaled smoke.

Perfect Moment

Complete stillness.
My legs extended
on easy chair
crossed at the ankles
knees a perfect pillow
for lap dog.
Together we sit
in this symbiotic pose
each taking solace
from the other.
No noise from electronics.
Nothing.
The quiet is intruded
by the dryer alarm.
Fifteen pound
fur ball's sleep
must be interrupted
to retrieve
the wife's towels.
The perfect moment lost
to the sound of her
disappointment, if I don't.

At the Assisted Living Facility

Like sunflowers opening to the sun
tiny, bent over people rise to my voice.
Eyes open, backs straighten
false teeth shine in smile
respond to a single, "Hello."

Hallway dimmer than actual light
arriving at the last room she'll ever know
she does not know us, not at first,
"Julie, you are so beautiful.
Oh look, my little altar boy."

Irish Alzheimer's (forget everything but
resentments) sucks like a vapor
out into the hall and out the doorway.
Sweet, little, (very little) old lady now sits
atop a single bed that seems to swallow her.

Shrunken as if she'd been left in the dryer
too long after a hot water wash.
Gone are the jowls, heavy hips that hurt her
back, replaced with bird bones as hollow
as her short-term memory.

Years of conflict, heavy weights heap atop
the family's shoulders, now just a fog.
Narcissism negates by nod of approval.
This visit, her sentence of solitude paroles
by her new digs at the memory care unit.

Fulgurite Rhythms

I want to get struck by lightning
      now that would be a way to go
leave my mark upon the ground
      so that everyone would know,

that I'd been here walking around
      dancing on this earth
I ended it with a flash
      in this fulgurited berth.

It's better than the outline
      drawn in policeman's chalk
mine is burned forever
      won't wear out when you walk.

I want to get struck by lightning
      the paper would do the story
maybe make the front page, too
      a reported blaze of glory.

The film would be at eleven
      the story precedes the weather
"The storm it was a freak one,
      tomorrow will be better."

I'd be gone, yesterday's news
      my impression left behind.
When the angels come to find me
      I won't be hard to find.

I want to get struck by lightning
      to be hit by a cosmic dart
have God aiming at me
      paint a target on my heart,

to be taken away from here like that
      beamed up to the sky
a million mega-watted burst
      brilliant way to say good bye.

39

Tom Cassidy Died Today

Tom Cassidy died today.
Blondest black man I ever knew.
Memories of meetings in May.
Softball at Croissant Park,
teeing it up at Rolling Hills
his stories of Southeast Asia,
smuggling, prison, bribery.

Tom Cassidy died today.
He ran a nightclub when
nightclubs were cool.
He once stole a ring just
to get the jewel.
He went into trances,
made dances with Frances.
He made it all seem easy.

Tom Cassidy died today.
Heroin usually wins
If the thunder don't get you
then the lightning will,
sang Jerry Garcia.
Heroin got Uncle Jerry.
Heroin got Tom.
Tom Cassidy died today.

A Way to Go

Some will talk about the way we want to go.
In my sleep, a heart attack while playing golf,
during a drive-by shooting.

More often we talk about how we don't want to go.
Don't want to take that chemo stuff.
Don't want to be a burden to my family.
Don't want to die slowly.

We leave instructions
what we want done afterwards.
Buried next to my saintly mother.
Ashes spread out on the ocean.
Stick of dynamite up my ass, blown to the four winds.

Some choose how, Ernest Hemingway,
Freddie Prinze, Jim Morrison, Marilyn Monroe.
Then there was my father.
His instructions were to spread his ashes on
the fairways of Rolling Hills Country Club.
Everyone thought he was kidding, except me.

His emphysema advanced
his kidneys at zero function.
"What if I stop taking dialysis?" he asked.
"You'll die," said the doctor.
"Check, please," said my dad.
Everyone thought he was kidding,
except the doctor.

I Am

I'm not hungry not horny
not having a bad day
not hearing little voices
who are telling me to pray.

I'm not hot not cold
not even feeling old
not angry not lonely
no one's left me stuck on hold.

I'm not working on my problems
not deep in therapy
not overly concerned
you'll be judging me.

Not upset by the congressmen
the parliament of whores
or the photographs on YouTube
that shows them on all fours.

I'm not worried this will end
this feeling which is good
not caring if this poem
winds up misunderstood.

I'm not concerned about tomorrow
living in today
caring about others
forgetting yesterday.

I am grateful for this feeling
happy it is here
sure it will continue
if I don't give in to fear.

I'm not hungry I'm not angry
not lonely, tired, too
I am grateful I can say
this is something new.

About the Author

Tonn Pastore has lived at the beach for twenty-three years because that's where they keep the ocean. This time allowed him to witness many changes. The influx of culture and the migration of people energized the slow pace of Jacksonville. The ocean breezes thinned not just the air around him but also the barriers around his heart. He married a third-generation native who showed him the joys of Jacksonville and the love of a new family. His poems pull from the pain and the joy of life and loss.

www.ingramcontent.com/pod-product-compliance
Lightning Source LLC
Chambersburg PA
CBHW060622030426
42337CB00018B/3149